THE LITTLE BOOK OF

Christmas Joys

H. Jackson Brown, Jr.,
Rosemary Brown, and Kathy Peel

RUTLEDGE HILL PRESS ● Nashville, Tennessee

Published in Nashville, Tennessee, by Rutledge Hill Press, Inc.,
211 Seventh Avenue North, Nashville, Tennessee 37219.
Distributed in Canada by H. B. Fenn and Company, Ltd., 1090 Lorimar Drive,
Mississauga, Ontario.

Typography by D&T/Bailey Typesetting, Inc., Nashville, Tennessee
Design by Bruce Gore, Gore Studio, Inc.

Library of Congress Cataloging-in-Publication Data

Brown, H. Jackson, 1940–
    The little book of christmas joys / by H. Jackson Brown, Jr.,
Rosemary Brown, Kathy Peel.
        p.   cm.
    ISBN 1-55853-310-9 (pbk.)
    1. Christmas.   I. Brown, Rosemary, 1945–   II. Peel, Kathy, 1951–   III. Title.
GT4985.B726   1994
394.2'663—dc20   94-30410
                                                                                    CIP

Printed in the United States of America
1 2 3 4 5 6 7 8 9 — 98 97 96 95 94

Introduction

ON A FROSTY December evening, my wife, Rosemary, and I and our friends the Peels were enjoying mugs of steaming spiced cider while watching the holiday classic, *It's a Wonderful Life*. A softly crackling fire silhouetted the Christmas stockings hanging from the mantel as we savored every familiar line until the movie reached its joyful ending. For fifteen years, hot cider, good friends, and *It's a Wonderful Life* have been the traditional ways my family has welcomed the Christmas season.

As I tossed another log on the fire, the four of us reminisced about the cherished Christmas traditions our families had maintained and the new ones we had lovingly created. We marveled at the power of holiday traditions and the comfort and continuity they bring to us each year.

We decided to pool our experiences into a collection of familiar and unique ways that our families and others have learned to *make it*

Christmas. And so, there in front of a crackling Christmas fire, the idea for *The Little Book of Christmas Joys* was formed.

It is the excitement and anticipation of favorite holiday traditions that help make this the most joyful time of the year. Even a small child senses something wonderful is about to happen when attic stairs are pulled down, dark recesses of closets are explored, and the search begins for holiday decorations that have been hibernating since last year. Our homes take on a distinctive fragrance as the halls are decked with fresh greenery and kitchens yield themselves to enthusiastic efforts and friendly disorder. Refrains from familiar carols fill the air with joy to the world as families are reunited and old friends embraced. Hope is renewed for peace on earth as we remember a baby born two thousand years ago.

It is our hope that *The Little Book of Christmas Joys* will bring an extra measure of joy to your holidays. You might discover, as we did, that joy almost always comes as a result of giving—giving gifts, giving hugs, giving help, giving a second chance, giving encouragement, and giving of ourselves.

Perhaps our thoughts will remind you of some old traditions you need to revive or some fresh new ideas you might want to try. But remember, the most treasured Christmas traditions develop slowly. Like the roasting holiday turkey, there's no need to hurry them along. So relax and let yourself enjoy the season of seasons.

From our homes to yours, we wish you the merriest and most joyful holiday ever. And may the blessing of Christmas traditions bring hope, love, and joy to each day of your New Year.

H. J. B.
Tall Pine Lodge
Fernvale, Tennessee

Other books by H. Jackson Brown, Jr.

A Father's Book of Wisdom
P.S. I Love You
Life's Little Instruction Book
Live and Learn and Pass It On
Life's Little Instruction Book, Volume II
Life's Little Treasure Book on Joy
Life's Little Treasure Book on Marriage and Family
Life's Little Treasure Book on Wisdom
Life's Little Treasure Book on Success
Wit & Wisdom from the Peanut Butter Gang

1 ◆ Be the first to wish everyone you meet a Merry Christmas.

2 ◆ Buy a pair of red flannel pajamas that you wear only on Christmas Eve.

3 ◆ Take the family to see a small town Christmas parade.

4 ◆ Don't count calories from December 15th through January 2nd.

5 ◆ Never select a Christmas tree after dark.

6 ◆ Mend a broken relationship with a friend or relative during the holidays.

7 ◆ Take a basket of Christmas goodies to a notoriously grumpy neighbor.

8 ◆ Be nice to sales personnel. They're often wearier than you are.

9 ◆ Don't schedule yourself too tightly during the holidays. Before making an appointment, ask yourself, "Can this wait until after Christmas?"

10 ◆ Take a holiday family photograph each year in the same spot, such as by a favorite tree in your yard. In years to come, you'll have a wonderful record of the growth of your family, as well as of the growth of the tree.

11 ◆ Find out what's on everyone's Christmas wish list when the family is together at Thanksgiving.

12 ◆ Make an effort to attend every Christmas party you're invited to, even if you can stay only a few minutes.

13 ◆ Place your children's stuffed animals under the Christmas tree as a welcoming committee for Santa.

14 ◆ Adopt a needy family for the holidays. Let members of your family buy a present for the person closest to their own age.

15 ◆ Fill your house with the holiday fragrance of cloves, orange peel, and cinnamon sticks simmering on the kitchen stove.

16 ◆ Don't despair if you are short of cash. Be creative. Looking back, you'll discover that the Christmases when you had the least money were the ones that left you with the best memories.

17 ◆ Ask your mother to send you the Christmas stocking you used when you were a kid and a couple of old family Christmas photos.

18 ◆ Let go of a problem you can't solve. Enjoy the season.

19 ◆ Hang a favorite Christmas tree ornament from your car's rear-view mirror.

20 ◆ Sprinkle red and green confetti in your Christmas card envelopes.

21 ◆ Introduce a child to the wonders of snowflakes. Chill a dark sheet of construction paper and then examine the flakes with a magnifying glass.

22 ◆ Bake Christmas cookies while a Johnny Mathis Christmas album plays in the background.

23 ◆ Take a few minutes each month to jot down your family's news. This will make writing your Christmas letter a lot easier.

24 ◆ Take a basket of Christmas goodies to your local fire and police stations.

25 ◆ Wear a smile and a Santa hat when you walk through the mall.

26 ◆ Early in December ask a camera store clerk to check your camera's battery.

27 ◆ If your child gives you a handmade gift, convince him it's your favorite gift of all.

28 ◆ Take along your address book when Christmas shopping so that you can ship out-of-town purchases directly from the store.

29 ◆ Be considerate of your in-laws' special Christmas traditions.

30 ◆ Purchase a special Christmas sweater and wear it often.

31 ◆ Choose a Christmas tree that's a little too big for the room.

32 ◆ Tie a wreath with a big, red bow to the grill of your car.

33 ◆ "It Smells Like Christmas" Pumpkin Bread

Christmas just wouldn't be Christmas without Pumpkin Bread. If you use disposable aluminum pans, it makes gift-giving even easier.

Yield: 2 (9x5x3 inch) loaves   Oven: 350°

3½ cups sifted all-purpose flour
2 teaspoons baking soda
1½ teaspoons salt
1 teaspoon baking powder
2 teaspoons cinnamon
2 teaspoons nutmeg
1 teaspoon allspice (optional)

½ teaspoon ground cloves
3 cups sugar
⅔ cup water
1 cup oil
5 eggs, beaten
1 16-ounce can pumpkin
1 cup chopped pecans

Grease two 9x5x3-inch loaf pans. In a large bowl mix together all of the dry ingredients. Blend in the water and oil, and mix in the eggs. Blend in the pumpkin. Fold in the pecans. Divide the batter between the prepared pans. Bake at 350° for 1 hour, or until a toothpick inserted in the center comes out clean.

34 ◆ Have a special place to display the Christmas card from the farthest distance away.

35 ◆ Organize a neighborhood progressive holiday dinner. Have appetizers at one home, the main course at another, and dessert at a third.

36 ◆ Try at least one new recipe and one new decorating idea.

37 ◆ Start working on a Christmas-themed jigsaw puzzle the first of December. Try to have it finished by Christmas Eve.

38 ◆ Take a shut-in a scrumptious Christmas dinner.

39 ◆ Rent a Santa Claus suit. Slip it on during your lunch hour and hand out candy canes to everyone in the office.

40 ◆ Hire high school or college students to help with your holiday entertaining. They can help serve, clean up before and after the party, and perform any number of odd jobs.

41 ◆ If you are short on space, set up a card table and cover it with a plaid tablecloth that reaches to the floor. Tuck all your gift-wrapping supplies under the table.

42 ◆ Take your family to a live performance of *The Nutcracker Suite.*

43 ◆ Take your family to a church choir's performance of Handel's *Messiah.*

44 ◆ Before going to bed on Christmas Eve, read by candlelight about the birth of Jesus in Luke, chapter 2. Then join hands with your family and sing "Silent Night."

45 ◆ Personalize your Christmas cards with a short hand-written note.

46 ◆ Don't forget our feathered friends during the holidays. Spread peanut butter on pine cones, then roll them in bird seed, and hang them on a tree near your kitchen window.

47 ◆ Tie jingle bells on your kid's shoelaces.

48 ◆ When you think you have enough lights on your tree, add two more strands.

49 ◆ Throw restraint to the wind. Christmas is the one time of year when bigger is better and gaudy is good.

50 ◆ Don't wait until Christmas Eve to wrap gifts. Wrap them as you purchase them.

51 ◆ Give a young member of your family the honor of placing the star or angel on top of the tree.

52 ◆ When sending a perishable food gift, schedule the delivery date when you know the recipient will be at home or at work to receive it.

53 ◆ Go caroling.

54 ◆ Avoid backtracking when doing your holiday shopping. Be sure you've finished in one department or store before you move on to the next.

55 ◆ Instead of the usual bedtime stories, read to your children about the Christmas customs in other countries.

56 ◆ Check for loose or burned-out bulbs *before* you put the strands of lights on the tree.

57 ◆ Buy more Scotch tape, wrapping paper, and enclosure cards than you think you'll need.

58 ◆ Lists help you get organized. Sit down on the Sunday afternoon after Thanksgiving and make lists of gifts you want to give, supplies you need to purchase, Christmas goodies you will prepare, and people you would like to entertain over the holidays.

59 ◆ Deliver delicious coffee cakes to your neighbors to enjoy on Christmas morning.

60 ◆ Never write the word *Christmas* as *Xmas*.

61 ◆ Enjoy a couple of meals illuminated only by the Christmas tree.

62 ◆ Recycle. Instead of throwing away wrinkled ribbon, run it through a curling iron to straighten it out. Use wrinkled wrapping paper as packing material.

63 ◆ Rosemary's Cranberry Salad

Even if it's not your turn to cook the holiday dinner, you'll probably have requests to fix this treat just to serve with turkey sandwiches. To make relish instead of congealed salad, leave out the unflavored gelatin and ½ cup of orange juice.

Yield: 16 to 20 servings

---

1 pound cranberries
4 oranges, one unpeeled
1 15-ounce can crushed pineapple
   packed in juice

2 cups sugar
½ cup orange juice
3 envelopes unflavored gelatin
½ pound pecans

Wash and sort the berries. Peel all but one orange and cut up all of the oranges. In a food grinder or food processor grind the cranberries and oranges. Add the drained pineapple, reserving the juice. Stir in the sugar and mix well. In a small saucepan combine the reserved pineapple juice and orange juice. Sprinkle the gelatin on top and stir. Heat until the gelatin is completely dissolved. Add the gelatin to the fruit mixture. Fold in the nuts. Pour into a greased 3-quart mold. (A Bundt pan makes a pretty mold.) Chill until set. Unmold onto a serving dish and serve with mayonnaise.

64 ◆ If you're feeling overwhelmed, break down big holiday projects into manageable tasks. For example, divide the number of Christmas cards you want to send by ten, and address one-tenth of the list each day for ten days.

65 ◆ During the year, collect inexpensive antique napkins at flea markets and yard sales. Use them to line baskets of Christmas goodies.

66 ◆ Take pictures after you've finished decorating your home. Not only will they be fun to look at later on, but you will have a visual reminder to help you decorate next year.

67 ◆ Try to finish your Christmas shopping by December 10.

68 ◆ Try to have all Christmas packages mailed by December 12th.

69 ◆ Before going to bed every night of the Christmas season, ask yourself, "Whose life did I make brighter today?"

70 ◆ Volunteer as a family to work in a soup kitchen or homeless shelter during the holidays.

71 ◆ Remind newlyweds to save an item from their wedding ceremony to use as a treasured Christmas ornament.

72 ◆ Send a Christmas basket to a college student the first of December. Include a Christmas music cassette or CD, decorations for the dorm room, Christmas cards, stamps, and a red pen.

73 ◆ Remember the three rules for reducing holiday hassles: (1) Plan ahead; (2) Begin early; (3) Keep it simple.

74 ◆ Don't give anyone a fruitcake.

75 ◆ Don't give a child underwear.

76 ◆ Don't give your spouse a bathroom scale.

77 ◆ Call a nursing home and get the names of five people who don't often receive mail. Send each one a beautiful Christmas card. Sign it, "from Santa."

78 ◆ Tip someone who doesn't expect it.

79 ◆ Wait until Christmas morning to place the infant Jesus in your Nativity scene.

80 ◆ Remember that the best solution for holiday blues is to do something special for someone else.

81 ◆ Tell your children about Christmas when you were their age.

82 ◆ Wear a colorful Christmas tie to holiday parties.

83 ◆ Wear outrageous Christmas socks.

84 ◆ Give new friends who have just moved to town a newspaper subscription from their old hometown.

85 ◆ Buy Christmas mugs for everyone in the family.

86 ◆ Sleep under a homemade quilt on Christmas Eve.

87 ◆ Watch *It's a Wonderful Life.*

88 ◆ Watch Albert Finney in *Scrooge.*

89 ◆ Watch "Frosty the Snowman."

90 ◆ Never refuse a holiday dessert.

91 ◆ Offer to run Christmas errands for an elderly friend or relative.

92 ◆ Give someone with failing eyesight the large-print edition of a classic book.

93 ◆ Cut off the fronts of attractive Christmas cards to use as gift tags.

94 ◆ Record a cheerful Christmas greeting for your answering machine.

95 ◆ Attend a Christmas Eve candlelight or watch night service with your family.

96 ◆ Remember your milkman, letter carrier, sanitation workers, and delivery people with a gift of cash.

97 ◆ Make snow angels.

98 ◆ Learn to say Merry Christmas in several languages.

99 ◆ Design and mail a homemade Christmas card to each member of the family.

100 ◆ Attend a church Christmas bazaar. Buy something whether you need it or not.

101 ◆ Send a couple of good friends a pre-Christmas musical gift of Harry Connick Jr.'s *When My Heart Finds Christmas*.

102 ◆ Begin a family Christmas journal. Write down memories your family shares: events you attend, presents you give and receive, and the inevitable crises that occur.

103 ◆ Buy a hot glue gun to help in creating holiday decorations.

104 ◆ Give an anonymous gift of money to someone who has been laid off.

105 ◆ Start a special collection for each of your children, adding one item each Christmas.

106 ◆ Ask for a gift box for each gift you buy.

107 ◆ Help an elderly neighbor decorate his or her home.

108 ◆ Curl up before an open fire with someone you love.

109 ◆ Remember that the more a toy costs, the more likely kids will want to play with the box it came in.

110 ◆ When a family member looks really stressed out, give them a big hug.

111 ◆ Stock up on staples and nonperishable foods you'll need for the holidays before the crowds get heavy at the supermarket.

112 ◆ On Christmas morning, phone some relatives who live far away and wish them a Merry Christmas.

113 ◆ Help your children bake Christmas breads or cookies to give to teachers, coaches, and school bus drivers.

114 ◆ Display prominently the Christmas artwork your child brings home from school.

115 ◆ If there's a model train in the attic or basement, get it out and set it up under the tree.

116 ◆ Santa's Thumbprint Cookies

Even a very young cook can have a "hands-on" experience making thumbprints in these delicious cookies.

Yield: about 3 dozen cookies   Oven: 375°

---

1 cup butter	2 cups all-purpose flour
⅔ cup sugar	3 tablespoons poppy seeds
2 egg yolks	Currant or strawberry jelly
1 teaspoon vanilla extract	White decorator's icing

In a large bowl cream the butter with an electric mixer at medium speed. Add the sugar, beating until light and fluffy. Beat in the egg yolks and vanilla. Gradually beat in the flour and poppy seeds. Wrap the dough in plastic wrap. Refrigerate for 1 to 2 hours, until chilled.

Shape the dough into 1-inch balls. Place on ungreased cookie sheets, about 2 inches apart. Press the center of each cookie with a thumb to form indentations. Bake at 375° for 12 to 14 minutes, or until lightly browned. Remove to wire racks to cool. Press the indentations again while the cookies are still warm. Just before serving, spoon jelly into the indentations and decorate with icing. Store in an airtight container.

117 ◆ Videotape family members recalling their favorite Christmas memories.

118 ◆ Unplug the Christmas lights before going to bed or leaving your house.

119 ◆ At least once in your life, visit New York and take in the Radio City Music Hall Christmas Show and enjoy the skaters and the huge Christmas tree at Rockefeller Plaza.

120 ◆ Buy a big wall calendar in December. Ask family members to write down their activities, so there won't be any mix-ups.

121 ◆ Never give your credit card number over the phone unless you initiated the call.

122 ◆ Relax with your family Christmas afternoon by looking at photos and videos from past Christmases.

123 ◆ Listen to the Barking Dogs "sing" "Jingle Bells." Once.

124 ◆ Before you buy any item over $25, check into the store's return policy.

125 ◆ Take a batch of Christmas goodies to the office for your co-workers to enjoy.

126 ◆ Put something Christmasy in every room of your home.

127 ◆ Remember that Christmas carols never sound better than when you sing them in church.

128 ◆ Take photos of your child's Christmas program. Have extra prints made for parents who could not attend.

129 ◆ End an evening with family and close friends by forming a circle, holding hands, and singing a favorite carol.

130 ◆ Take the family out to eat at the same restaurant every year before picking out and bringing home the Christmas tree.

131 ◆ Don't shop during peak hours. Avoid lunchtime and Saturdays; early mornings and evenings are best.

132 ◆ Don't wait until 1:30 A.M. Christmas morning to start putting together "Some Assembly Required" toys.

133 ◆ If you enjoy cooking, bake double batches of Christmas goodies for your friends who might be too busy to cook.

134 ◆ Enjoy Christmas music in your home, office, and car to keep you in the holiday spirit.

135 ◆ When you don't know what to give, give a book. Inscribe it with your name, the occasion, and the date.

136 ◆ Sometime during the holidays, thumb through the toy section of an old Sears and Roebuck catalog.

137 ◆ Fill a basket with photos from past Christmases. Put it in a prominent spot.

138 ◆ Buy only approved weatherproof lights and extension cords for outside use. Wrap the connection with plastic electrical tape.

139 ◆ Whistle "Walking in a Winter Wonderland" in the shower.

140 ◆ Organize a neighborhood yard decorating contest with the winner receiving a plate of goodies from the losers.

141 ◆ Never set a candle on a counter underneath a cabinet or a shelf. Heat rises and can create a fire hazard.

142 ◆ Create a homemade sled from a large appliance box. Then look for the biggest hill you can find.

143 ◆ Be creative with gift wrapping. Use old maps, the funny papers, posters, the yellow pages.

144 ◆ Consider buying your Christmas tree from the Boy Scouts or a service organization's tree lot.

145 ◆ Ask your local post office for its recommended mailing deadline dates for packages and letters.

146 ◆ Don't send Christmas cash in the mail.

147 ◆ Some time during the holidays, go through your closets and box up clothing you haven't worn in two years. Give away items that are still in good condition.

148 ◆ To save time, sit back and do some of your shopping from catalogs. Here are some of our favorites:

Wireless: (800) 669–9999
   Whimsical merchandise, Midwestern apparel, books, music, nostalgia
Sundance: (800) 225–5592
   Southwestern hand-crafted items
Smith & Hawken: (800) 383–2000
   Gardening supplies
Crate & Barrel: (800) 323–1781
   Housewares
Exposures: (800) 572–5750
   Photography equipment, frames, lighting, storage albums
Community Kitchens: (800) 535–9901
   Kitchen utensils, Louisianan-Cajun food, coffee

Horchow Collection: (800) 456–7000
   Home items, decoratives, women's apparel, furniture
Museum of Modern Art Design Store: (800) 447–6662
   Posters, furniture, umbrellas, Christmas cards, ties
Harry & David: (800) 345–5655
   Fruits, vegetables, plants, bakery items, chocolate
Hold Everything: (800) 421–2264
   Home organizational materials
Jardine's Texas Foods: (800) 544–1880
   Specialty foods, sauces, barbecue sauce, salad dressings
Museum of Fine Art Boston: (800) 225–5592
   Reproductions of art and jewelry in the museum collection
The "You Are Loved" Custom Cookie Company
(800) 458–3596
   A variety of home-baked cookies packed in pretty tins
Early's Honey Stand: (800) 523–2015
   Smoked meats, jams, jellies

149 ◆ Wish someone a happy holiday with music. Dial 1–800–422–SONG and Send-A-Song will deliver your specially selected Christmas song and recorded personal greeting over the phone.

150 ◆ Line your walk or driveway with luminaries made from paper bags filled with two inches of sand with a votive candle set in the center.

151 ◆ Record names and addresses in your address book as you receive Christmas cards—before you throw away the envelopes.

152 ◆ When you're with a child and see a blinking red light in the sky, ask her, "Do you think that could be Rudolph?"

153 ◆ Allow extra time to navigate through Christmas traffic.

154 ◆ The week before Christmas, talk with your children about the first Christmas and how the birth of Jesus has affected the world.

155 ◆ Offer refreshments to carolers when they come to your door.

156 ◆ Christmas Eve day, listen on NPR to a special musical program from King's College Chapel, Cambridge.

157 ◆ Create a special Christmas morning breakfast menu and serve it every year.

158 ◆ Save a copy of your children's letters to Santa. Put them in a scrapbook to enjoy for years to come.

159 ◆ If your parents live far away, videotape your family trimming the tree and decorating your home and send it to them to enjoy Christmas Day.

160 ◆ Take the initiative. Don't wait for someone else to spread Christmas joy.

161 ◆ Take turns opening presents on Christmas morning. When the gift is an article of clothing, it's always fun to ask the recipient to model it.

162 ◆ Have a florist deliver a Christmas arrangement to a favorite long-distance relative or friend.

163 ♦ Throughout the holiday season, give your family the gift of a sweet disposition.

164 ◆ Help your child make red and green paper chains from construction paper. Hang them all over her bedroom.

165 ◆ Tie a red plaid bow on your pet's collar.

166 ◆ Try the Swedish custom of writing a short, lighthearted poem on your gift card that half reveals the contents of the package.

167 ◆ Reserve a night for the entire family to make homemade ornaments for your tree.

168 ◆ If a Christmas party requires a tuxedo, wear a sprig of holly as a boutonniere.

169 ◆ Stock your freezer with meals for the holidays by doubling or tripling recipes for spaghetti sauce, casseroles, and other foods that freeze well.

170 ◆ Make sure that salespeople tear up the carbons of your charge-card purchases.

171 ◆ Offer to help a disabled person with his or her Christmas shopping.

172 ◆ Call the Land O' Lakes holiday bakeline at (800) 782–9606 for any questions regarding baking.

173 ◆ Set aside some time at the beginning of the holiday season to help your children plan their gift-giving lists.

174 ◆ Give your place in the gift-wrapping line to someone who looks as if she has had a hard day.

175 ◆ As hectic as the holidays are, try to keep up with your regular fitness routine.

176 ◆ When attending holiday parties, don't
arrive earlier than you were invited,
and don't be the last to leave.

177 ◆ Wrap your child's bedroom door with
pretty gift paper to transform it into a
giant package.

178 ◆ Invite a friend who doesn't have a
church home to a special service at
your church.

179 ◆ Ask the price of custom gift wrapping *before* you leave the gift to be wrapped. It's often very expensive.

180 ◆ Offer to baby-sit for new parents to give them a chance to do some shopping.

181 ◆ When decorating the tree, nestle photos of past Christmas trees in the branches.

182 ◆ Compliment at least three people every day in December. This is a gift that's always appreciated.

183 ◆ Tape Christmas cards around a doorway so you can enjoy them each time you walk into the room.

184 ◆ Take some time out to sit in the mall and watch youngsters having their pictures made with Santa.

185 ◆ Remember the bubble lights your parents used to decorate Christmas trees when you were young? They are available again. Buy a couple of strands for old time's sake.

186 ◆ Don't forget the ornament hooks.

187 ◆ Don't forget the extension cords.

188 ◆ Don't forget the eggnog.

189 ◆ To help it stay fresh, saw an inch off the bottom of your Christmas tree before placing it in the stand. Check the water level every day.

190 ◆ Give your Christmas tree a second life by having it ground into garden mulch.

191 ◆ Include a family photo with Christmas cards sent to relatives and friends you don't see often.

192 ◆ Let a child decorate a small Christmas tree just the way he likes it for his bedroom.

193 ◆ Don't leave packages in plain view when you park your car. Store them in the trunk.

194 ◆ When older children come home for the holidays, remember that they need some privacy and breathing space.

195 ◆ Let the youngest and oldest family members pass out the presents.

196 ◆ Start a collection of Christmas cookie cutters.

197 ◆ Refuse to let heavy traffic and long lines dampen your Christmas spirit.

198 ◆ Wear a Christmas apron while cooking in the kitchen during December.

199 ◆ Store holiday candles in a cool, dry place. Never put them next to linens; the dye may fade onto the fabric.

200 ◆ After attending a holiday party, be sure to call or write the host to say "thank you" for a wonderful time.

201 ◆ Fix yourself a cup of hot cocoa and read "Stopping by Woods on a Snowy Evening" by Robert Frost.

202 ◆ Never give a gift that's not nicely wrapped.

203 ◆ Give a donation every time you pass a Salvation Army bell-ringer.

204 ◆ Put white twinkle lights on your large house plants.

205 ◆ Have a special outfit or accessory that you wear only on Christmas day.

206 ◆ Regardless of the temperature, if you have a fireplace, have it blazing Christmas Eve and Christmas Day.

207 ◆ Wrap a gift in an odd-shaped package so the recipient can't guess what it is.

208 ◆ If you have small children or pets, be careful when decorating with greenery that has poisonous leaves or berries, such as poinsettias, holly, and mistletoe.

209 ◆ Make a friend of an
enemy this Christmas.

210 ◆ On a clear night, find the bright North Star and recall the story of the Wise Men.

211 ◆ Teach children to look at the gift tag *before* they open the present so they will know whom to thank.

212 ◆ Don't burn wrapping paper in the fireplace. It's a fire and a health hazard.

213 ◆ Be a generous giver.

214 ◆ Be a gracious receiver.

215 ◆ Make it a daily practice during the holiday season to do something nice for someone without telling them you did it.

216 ◆ Read "'Twas the Night Before Christmas" the night before Christmas.

217 ◆ Send Christmas cards with encouraging messages to military personnel on duty overseas.

218 ◆ Record your young child singing Christmas carols on a cassette tape. Send it to grandparents who live far away.

219 ◆ Be the first to lob a snowball and start a battle.

220 ◆ Set out a bowl of walnuts, tangerines, and pecans in the family room.

221 ◆ Buy a big red candle for the kitchen table. Light it every night at dinner during the holidays.

222 ◆ Attend a children's Christmas pageant.

223 ◆ Keep a fire extinguisher near the tree and in the kitchen.

224 ◆ Decorate your living room or family room with a pot of fragrant paper whites.

225 ◆ Welcome a new family to your neighborhood with a plate of Christmas goodies.

226 ◆ Never give a gift to someone else's child that you wouldn't want your own child to receive.

227 ◆ Open Christmas cards as a family activity each night at the dinner table. Read the messages aloud.

228 ◆ Give someone who's discouraged the gift of encouragement.

229 ◆ Make your family feel just as important as your holiday company.

230 ◆ Pay a debt for someone.

231 ◆ Add a new Christmas cassette or CD to your music collection each year.

232 ◆ Offer to carry someone's packages.

233 ◆ Plan a quiet evening with your family the week after Christmas. Talk about your goals for the coming year.

234 ◆ Take your family and some neighborhood children ice skating.

235 ◆ Ruth's World Class Pralines

These pralines make a wonderful gift for friends. But you may need to hide them to keep family members from devouring them before you can give them away.

Yield: 12 to 15 pralines

---

2 cups sugar
⅛ teaspoon salt
1 teaspoon baking soda
1 cup buttermilk

2 tablespoons butter
1½ cups pecan halves
1 teaspoon vanilla

In a large, heavy saucepan combine the sugar, salt, baking soda, and buttermilk. Bring to a boil quickly, stirring constantly, until mixture turns a creamy beige (about 210°). Add the butter and pecans and cook over medium heat, stirring frequently, to the soft ball stage (234°–240°). Remove the pan from the heat and add the vanilla. Beat with a spoon until the mixture loses its gloss. Drop into mounds on waxed paper, working as quickly as you can, since the mixture thickens fast.

236 ◆ Load the family in the car, slip in your favorite Christmas tape, and drive through the neighborhood looking at the Christmas decorations. Roll down the windows and shout, "Merry Christmas" to everyone you see.

237 ◆ Anonymously send someone who's wronged you a Christmas card with a sincere wish for happiness and well-being.

238 ◆ Serve holiday cookies on a Santa Claus platter.

239 ◆ Give a small gift—such as a tree ornament—to each guest when you have a holiday party.

240 ◆ If you're feeling harried, go to a church, sit in the sanctuary, and reflect on the real meaning of Christmas. You'll leave feeling more peaceful.

241 ◆ Host a holiday reception for a friend who's started a new business.

242 ◆ Use festive holiday postage stamps on envelopes and packages.

243 ◆ Consider taking a family trip one Christmas instead of exchanging gifts.

244 ◆ Introduce a shy person to others at the office Christmas party.

245 ◆ Toast your friends when they are in your home. Tell them how much it means to you to have them there.

246 ◆ Keep plenty of apple cider and microwave popcorn on hand for unexpected drop-in holiday guests.

247 ◆ Don't forget, no matter how many Christmas photos you take, next year you'll wish you had taken more.

248 ◆ Read to your family "The Gift of the Magi" by O. Henry.

249 ◆ This Christmas, write letters to several people who have had a positive influence on your life. Thank them for this gift they have given you.

250 ◆ Buy a book of Christmas carols and keep it open on the piano during the holidays.

251 ◆ Put Christmas lights and a small wreath on the dog house.

252 ◆ Let someone else have the parking space you've just found. Think of it as a gift to a stranger.

253 ◆ When traveling, pick up small inexpensive souvenir items that can be used as tree ornaments. They will remind you of your happy travels.

254 ◆ Ask the oldest married man and the youngest married woman to pull the Christmas turkey wishbone.

255 ◆ Give gifts with no strings attached.

256 ◆ Write with a red or green pen during the holidays.

257 ◆ Tie peppermint candy canes to children's packages.

258 ◆ Buy something from students holding a Christmas bake sale and tell them to keep the change.

259 ◆ Don't give an errand along with a gift. Unless you're certain of the correct size, don't give someone clothing. Exchanging clothes is a hassle.

260 ◆ Take a child to the library and check out a book of Christmas stories.

261 ◆ Keep money in individual envelopes to give spontaneously to others when you're touched by the Christmas spirit.

262 ◆ Write a Christmas greeting at the top of your business faxes.

263 ◆ When holiday travels take you to cities where you have friends, call or write ahead and try to get together, even if it's for only a few minutes.

264 ◆ Include your children in the preparation of holiday meals. This teaches them skills they will need in years to come.

265 ◆ Add a note of appreciation to the Christmas card you give your child's teacher.

266 ◆ This season, cut others—as well as yourself—more slack than usual.

267 ◆ Replace your shoelaces with a red one and a green one.

268 ◆ Invest in an inexpensive postal scale. It can save you time waiting in line at the post office.

269 ◆ Put pebbles inside children's gift boxes so that when they shake the packages, they won't be able to guess what's inside.

270 ◆ If your child gets a new game for Christmas, play it with him and let him win.

271 ◆ When you put away the decorations, label each box. You'll have a better chance of starting the season with joy next year.

272 ◆ Stop and help someone who's stuck in the snow.

273 ◆ Take a decorated miniature Christmas tree to someone in a hospital or a nursing home.

274 ◆ As a courtesy to your neighbors, alert them before you have a large holiday party.

275 ◆ Be others-centered instead of self-centered. A person wrapped up in himself makes a very small package.

276 ◆ Take a walk with someone you love on Christmas afternoon.

277 ◆ Give tickets to a special Christmas performance to someone who couldn't otherwise afford to go.

278 ◆ Read *The Littlest Angel* by Charles Tazewell to a child.

279 ◆ Remember that the loving holiday spirit in your home depends more on the words you speak than on the gifts you give.

280 ◆ If someone disappoints you this season, don't give a lecture. Give acceptance and forgiveness.

281 ◆ Once or twice, take a different route home from work and enjoy the decorations in another neighborhood.

282 ◆ Turn off the lights and put on a recording of Bing Crosby's "White Christmas." Ask your spouse to dance.

283 ◆ Tour a historic home in your area that has been decorated for the holidays.

284 ◆ When you phone a store during the holidays, ask the clerk, "Are you with a customer or do you have time for me to ask you a question?"

285 ◆ Open Christmas gifts with your favorite Christmas music playing in the background.

286 ◆ Secretly shovel the snow off your neighbor's front walk.

287 ◆ Answer your phone by saying "Merry Christmas."

288 ◆ Throw orange or tangerine peels into your fire for a spicy aroma.

289 ◆ Write names and dates on the backs of holiday photographs.

290 ◆ Pray that God will help you see opportunities to be a blessing to others this Christmas.

291 ◆ If you are having trouble deciding on gifts to give young nieces, nephews, and other youngsters on your list, ask friends who have children of the same sex and age for ideas.

292 ◆ Save the receipts for every gift you buy.

293 ◆ Learn the names of Santa's reindeer.

294 ◆ Learn the second verse to "Jingle Bells."

295 ◆ Challenge someone to sing all the verses of "The Twelve Days of Christmas."

296 ◆ Create a gag gift that is passed on to different family members every Christmas. A complimentary hotel shower cap always brings lots of laughs.

297 ◆ Use candles safely: (1) Don't leave burning candles unattended; (2) Be sure the candle is firmly anchored to its holder; (3) Use the right size or type of holder for the candle.

298 ◆ Have an extra ice scraper to give to someone who might need one.

299 ◆ Pay baby sitters a little extra during the holidays.

300 ◆ When a child mentions something that he or she would like to receive as a gift, never say, "We'll see," if you have no intention of getting it.

301 ◆ Order two take-out lunches—one for yourself and one to give to a homeless person.

302 ◆ Buy Christmas gifts from local artists and craftsmen.

303 ◆ When you have friends over and there's Christmas magic in the air, don't let the evening end early. Throw another log on the fire.

304 ◆ Offer to keep a friend's children when you learn that their sitter has canceled right before a holiday party.

305 ◆ Pay the toll for the car behind you during the week of Christmas.

306 ◆ Carry jumper cables. If you don't need them, you're set to help someone else.

307 ◆ Order and pay for a pizza for a neighbor. Ask the delivery person to tell them it's from Santa.

308 ◆ Set aside twenty minutes each day to catch your breath. Make yourself a cup of tea, put your feet up, and turn on the answering machine.

309 ◆ If you take a trip by plane during the holidays, offer to trade seats so a family can sit together.

310 ◆ Let someone with just a few items go ahead of you in line at the grocery store.

311 ◆ Use poster board and felt-tipped markers to create a giant-size family Christmas card for someone special.

312 ◆ If you're including young children in your holiday open house, set up a separate area for them and enlist the help of a neighborhood high-school student to supervise.

313 ◆ Get the conversation started around the holiday dinner table by taking turns sharing "the Christmas I remember best," or "the craziest present I ever received."

314 ◆ Use package sealing tape—*not* string or twine— when sending packages. Tape won't get caught in machinery or conveyor belts.

315 ◆ Start a family tree-trimming tradition. Serve the same refreshments and play the same music every year.

316 ◆ At a holiday buffet, offer to go through the line for an older person.

317 ◆ When you hear the song "Rockin' Around the Christmas Tree," grab the family member closest to you and kick up your heels.

318 ◆ Order well in advance the special foods you need for holiday entertaining.

319 ◆ This Christmas, give yourself the gift of living in peace with those things you cannot change.

320 ◆ If you have children who are old enough to wrap their own gifts, provide them with their own supply of wrapping materials.

321 ◆ Serve some meals in front of the fire.

322 ◆ If you don't have extended family close by, invite a family with similar circumstances to share some Christmas festivities with you.

323 ◆ Smile at police officers, fire fighters, emergency personnel, and security guards. Thank them for being on the job during the holidays.

324 ◆ Consider hosting a holiday party the week after Christmas instead of trying to squeeze it in during the busy weeks before Christmas. Your house will still be decorated and it will be easier to relax and enjoy your guests.

325 ◆ Ask neighbors if you can watch their house, pick up their newspapers, and collect their mail when they are out of town during the holidays.

326 ◆ Let your child know you care about his or her world. Host a Christmas party for several school friends.

327 ◆ Give someone who's disappointed you the gift of a clean slate this Christmas.

328 ◆ Avoid misunderstandings during the holidays by trying to settle controversial family matters ahead of time.

329 ◆ During a long flight, offer to entertain a small child for a while for a parent traveling alone during the holidays.

330 ◆ Instead of wrapping packages, try putting gifts in decorative shopping bags filled with colorful tissue.

331 ◆ Holiday catalogs come earlier and earlier each year, but it's *never* too early to start ordering gifts and holiday goodies.

332 ◆ Instead of giving gifts at the office, take up a collection to give to a designated charity.

333 ◆ Don't let a rude person steal your Christmas joy.

334 ◆ Give a pint of blood;
it's the gift of life.

335 ◆ If you are planning a large holiday party, call early to reserve the equipment and supplies that need to be rented.

336 ◆ When you see a family or group taking holiday pictures of each other, offer to take one of the whole group.

337 ◆ Give children toys that encourage their creativity.

338 ◆ Avoid fruitless shopping trips. Call stores before you leave home to check on prices and availability of the items you plan to buy.

339 ◆ Trade out baking with three friends. Each of you bake double batches of your favorite recipes; then swap.

340 ◆ Give your seat on the bus or subway to someone holding lots of packages.

341 ◆ Let your children participate in decorating the house for Christmas. It's more important for them to help than for everything to look picture-perfect.

342 ◆ Don't purchase anything in a package that is damaged or looks like it has been opened.

343 ◆ Acknowledge every gift you receive.

344 ◆ Write "Joy to the World" with your finger on a frosty window pane.

345 ◆ Follow the Irish tradition of putting a bird's nest in your Christmas tree.

346 ◆ Instead of buying expensive holiday wrapping paper, purchase a large roll of plain brown kraft paper or white butcher paper and a large bolt of red plaid ribbon from a florist supply store.

347 ◆ Sometimes students who live long distances away can't afford to go home for the holidays. Call the dean of a local college and ask if there might be a couple of students who would like to share a holiday meal with your family.

348 ◆ If your office is at home, be realistic about how much you will be able to accomplish with the children out of school for the holidays.

349 ◆ *Amaretto Fudge Cake*

We would rather have this than Christmas fudge any day!

Yield: 24 large brownies (quite a few more "dainty" ones!)   Oven: 350°

1¾ cups butter, divided
1 cup cocoa, divided
4 eggs
2 cups granulated sugar
2 teaspoons vanilla extract

1 cup all-purpose flour
¼ teaspoon salt
1½ cups chopped nuts
2¼ cups confectioners' sugar
4 tablespoons Amaretto

In a saucepan melt 1¼ cups of butter. Remove the pan from the heat. Add ¾ cup of cocoa and beat until smooth. In a large mixing bowl beat the eggs until fluffy. Gradually beat in the sugar until the mixture is thick. Stir in the chocolate mixture and add the vanilla. Stir in the flour and salt and beat until smooth. Fold in the nuts. Spread the batter into a greased 10x15-inch pan. Bake at 350° for 30 minutes, or until firm. While the brownies are cooling, make the frosting by melting the remaining ½ cup of butter. Add the confectioners' sugar alternately with the Amaretto and beat until smooth. Beat in the remaining ¼ cup of cocoa and spread over the cooled brownies. Allow the brownies to cool thoroughly before cutting.

350 ◆ For a quick holiday centerpiece, fill a large bowl with red apples. Intersperse with sprigs of greenery.

351 ◆ Never prepare new recipes for holiday meals unless you've tried them out at least once beforehand.

352 ◆ Serve cinnamon sticks with hot cider and peppermint sticks with hot chocolate.

353 ◆ Buy a children's Christmas music tape or CD. Listen and sing along with your children while you're running errands together in the car.

354 ◆ Make sure your car battery is in good condition. A dead battery in a mall parking lot challenges even the brightest holiday spirit.

355 ◆ Let other cars pull in front of you.

356 ◆ Be sure to wave a "thank you" when somebody lets you into holiday traffic.

357 ◆ If one family member lives far away and can't afford to fly home, suggest that other family members chip in and buy him a ticket.

358 ◆ Take time to remember that the greatest gift is a home filled with the people you love.

359 ◆ Volunteer to deliver Meals on Wheels to shut-ins.

360 ◆ Ask children, "What are you *giving* for Christmas?" instead of "What are you *getting* for Christmas?"

361 ◆ If you have friends who have lost family members since last Christmas, make a special effort to call and cheer them during the holidays.

362 ◆ Have a special Christmas tablecloth that's used only on Christmas Day.

363 ◆ Holiday entertaining doesn't have to be elaborate or complicated. Just make a big pot of chili, toss a green salad, and bake a pan of brownies.

364 ◆ Get out old games—Monopoly, Clue, and Parcheesi—and have an ongoing family tournament during December.

365 ◆ Let younger children create their own Christmas wrapping paper with white paper and an assortment of rubber stamps and colored ink pads.

366 ◆ Christmas is the season for time-honored traditions. Don't attempt major changes.

367 ◆ Discover the quiet satisfaction of anonymous giving.

368 ◆ Avoid last-minute personal shopping. Decide ahead of time which clothes and accessories you will wear to holiday festivities.

369 ◆ Keep your holiday recipe collection in a special file or folder. Add to it each year.

370 ◆ Have a photo made of you and your family with Santa Claus.

371 ◆ Instead of exchanging gifts with close friends at Christmas, decide to take each other to lunch.

372 ◆ Take your camera to holiday parties. Send the photos to your host or hostess with your thank-you note.

373 ◆ Make arrangements to donate leftover food from a holiday party to a homeless shelter.

374 ◆ Save the original boxes for fragile Christmas decorations, so that you can pack them back securely after the holidays.

375 ◆ If you hide gifts, write down what you have hidden and where.

376 ◆ Keep up with the local news during the holiday season to learn if there is someone who might need your help.

377 ◆ If you are taking a car trip with children during the holidays, create silly new verses for "The Twelve Days of Christmas."

378 ◆ As you pack up the Christmas tree decorations, ask family members to write a prediction for the coming year on a piece of paper. Put them in the ornament box and read them next year.

379 ◆ Don't try to do everything yourself. Remember, even Santa needs helpers.

380 ◆ If a service club is selling poinsettia plants, buy some.

381 ◆ If you have young children, be sure to line up sitters well in advance for holiday events.

382 ◆ When you put away your Christmas lights, wrap each strand around a large empty gift box and slip a plastic bag over it.

383 ◆ The day you take down the holiday decorations, hold a family council and ask everyone what they liked best and least about the holidays.

384 ◆ Put your name and address and the recipient's name and address inside the package as well as outside when sending out-of-town Christmas gifts. If the package is damaged, there will still be a way to ensure its delivery.

385 ◆ Use a heavy plastic garbage can to store bulky Christmas decorations.

386 ◆ Put stockings filled with small gifts and treats on the back of dining chairs for friends when they come to your home for a holiday dinner.

387 ◆ When you are bidding your host good-bye at a Christmas party, don't linger at the door.

388 ◆ If you're cooking your first turkey this Christmas, and your mother or grandmother is not around to help, call the Turkey Talkline with your questions: (800) 323–4848.

389 ◆ Fill a pump-dispenser thermos with boiling water each morning as you're fixing breakfast. Then you'll be ready to fix a quick cup of instant cocoa or hot spiced tea for a drop-in guest.

390 ◆ Wrap a few small picture frames, fabric-covered blank books, or nonperishable food items for those you may have inadvertently left off your Christmas list. Put a blank gift tag on the package to be filled out later.

391 ◆ Make more space in your refrigerator for entertaining by temporarily transferring all the little bottles and jars into a picnic cooler.

392 ◆ Never wrap a gift in a box with a store's name on it unless the gift came from that store. It's confusing if the gift needs to be returned.

393 ◆ Save your gift lists from year to year. This will help avoid duplications and give you ideas for next year.

394 ◆ Keep all packing cartons in case you need to make returns.

395 ◆ When sending Christmas thank-you notes, tuck in a snapshot of yourself enjoying the gift.

396 ◆ Try to have Christmas thank-you notes written and mailed by January 15.

397 ◆ If you are having trouble deciding on some gifts to give, contact a department store and speak with a personal shopper. This service is free.

398 ◆ If your children are grown, offer to take one of your friend's small children out for a special holiday activity.

399 ◆ Research your family history and serve a special holiday food or drink that your ancestors might have enjoyed.

400 ◆ Amidst the hustle and bustle, the stress and the strain, take time to be good to yourself.

401 ◆ If you can't fit all your guests at one table for Christmas dinner, set up a second table in another room and have them exchange places between dinner and dessert.

402 ◆ Let the youngest child in the family who's old enough read the Christmas story on Christmas Eve. Record it on tape, and save it for them when they are grown.

403 ◆ Every year, buy a tree ornament for each of your children. Choose ones that represent important events that happened to them during the past year. When they move away from home, give them their collection of ornaments to put on their own tree.

404 ◆ Don't overwhelm youngsters by allowing them to open lots of presents in a short amount of time.

405 ◆ *Aunt Emma's Baked Apricots*

This is delicious with any traditional Christmas meal: turkey, ham, or goose. People always come back for seconds, so be sure to make plenty!

Yield: 8 servings   Oven: 300°

---

2 17-ounce cans apricot halves, drained
1 16-ounce can tart cherries, drained
1 cup brown sugar

8 ounces Ritz crackers (2 rolls)
¾ cup butter

Line a baking dish with 1 can of apricot halves and sprinkle ¼ cup of brown sugar over them. Add 2 ounces (½ tube) of crumbled Ritz crackers and dot with 3 tablespoons butter, cut into chunks. Next, add half the cherries, followed by another ¼ cup of brown sugar, ½ tube of Ritz crackers, and 3 tablespoons of butter. Make another layer with the second can of apricot halves, ¼ cup brown sugar, ½ tube of crumbled Ritz crackers, and 3 tablespoons of butter. Finish with the remaining cherries, brown sugar, Ritz crackers, and butter. Bake at 300° for 1 hour.

406 ◆ Offer to hide your neighbors' Christmas gifts for their children so that young snoopers won't discover them.

407 ◆ Mail in warranty cards promptly.

408 ◆ Hang up stockings for every member of the family. Don't forget the pets.

409 ◆ Watch the television special, "A Charlie Brown Christmas."

410 ◆ Send your Sunday school teacher a Christmas card and a note of appreciation.

411 ◆ For toys and appliances, save manufacturers' addresses, consumer-service information, and hotline numbers.

412 ◆ Everyone loves a teddy bear. Give at least one every Christmas.

413 ◆ Remember that peace on earth starts with peace in our homes and in our hearts.

414 ◆ Take your children with you when you make a cash donation to a homeless shelter or charity, and let them experience the joy of giving.

415 ◆ Don't use the words "I'm on a diet" during the holidays.

416 ◆ After opening the presents, hug all your family members and tell them they are the best gift of all.

417 ◆ The week after Christmas, help your children go through their toys and select some that are still in good condition to give to the less fortunate.

418 ◆ Never miss an opportunity to shake hands with Santa Claus.

419 ◆ If your family doesn't celebrate many Christmas traditions, let this be the year you create some.

420 ◆ For Christmas dinner, prepare as many do-ahead dishes as you can.

421 ◆ Turn down your thermostat before the guests arrive for a large holiday get-together. Crowded rooms heat up quickly.

422 ◆ Stock up on candles, Christmas cards, tree decorations, and paper goods at after-Christmas sales.

423 ◆ Feed someone's expired parking meter.

424 ◆ Don't expect your husband or wife to wear a halo during the holidays. Give your spouse the gift of patience, flexibility, and a sense of humor.

425 ◆ On New Year's Day, light three candles and think about the three things that happened the past year for which you are most thankful.

426 ◆ In addition to your regular Christmas card list, track down the addresses of a couple of people with whom you've lost touch and send them a Christmas greeting.

427 ◆ Save a length of Christmas tree trunk to burn as next year's yule log.

428 ◆ Look the other way when Grandma and Grandpa spoil your children.

429 ◆ Don't forget to put out Santa's milk and cookies.

430 ◆ Don't forget to hang the mistletoe.

431 ◆ Don't forget the batteries.

432 ◆ Don't forget whose birthday we're celebrating.

Dear Reader:

If you would like to share a couple of your
favorite family traditions or holiday ideas with us,
we'd love to hear from you.
Our address is:

CHRISTMAS JOYS
P.O. Box 150285
Nashville, TN 37215